HENRY FORD

Automotive Innovator

by Wil Mara

Content Consultant

Nanci R. Vargus, Ed.D.
Professor Emeritus, University of Indianapolis

Reading Consultant

Jeanne M. Clidas, Ph.D.
Reading Specialist

Children's Press®
An Imprint of Scholastic Inc.

Library of Congress Cataloging-in-Publication Data
Names: Mara, Wil, author.
Title: Henry Ford : automotive innovator/by Wil Mara.
Other titles: Rookie biography.
Description: New York, NY: Children's Press, an imprint of Scholastic Inc., 2018. |
Series: Rookie biographies | Includes bibliographical references and index.
Identifiers: LCCN 2016051658| ISBN 9780531232255 (library binding: alk. paper) |
ISBN 9780531238592 (pbk.: alk. paper)
Subjects: LCSH: Ford, Henry, 1863-1947—Juvenile literature. | Automobile industry and trade—
United States—Biography—Juvenile literature. | Industrialists—United States—Biography—Juvenile
literature. | Automobile engineers—United States—Biography—Juvenile literature.
Classification: LCC TL140.F6 M325 2018 | DDC 338.7/6292/092 [B]—dc23
LC record available at https://lccn.loc.gov/2016051658

Produced by Spooky Cheetah Press
Design by Judith Christ-Lafond
Poem by Jodie Shepherd

Printed in Malaysia 108

2 3 4 5 6 7 8 9 10 R 27 26 25 24 23 22 21 20 19

Photographs ©: cover main: Getty Images; cover background: bluebeat76/Getty Images; cover
bottom left: Mark Elias/Bloomberg/Getty Images; back cover: PhotoQuest/Getty Images; 3:
GraphicaArts/Getty Images; 4: Getty Images; 6: Hulton Archive/Getty Images; 8 top left: Everett
Collection Historical/Alamy Images; 8 main: Bettmann/Getty Images; 11: Apic/Getty Images; 12
-13: AP Images; 14: Rue des Archives/The Granger Collection; 17: Hulton Archive/Getty Images;
18: Underwood Archives/Getty Images; 21: Hulton Collection/Getty Images; 22: Sueddeutsche
Zeitung Photo/Alamy Images; 24: Corbis/Getty Images; 27: Bettmann/Getty Images; 29: Imagno/
Getty Images; 30 background: Hulton Archive/Getty Images; 31 center bottom: Hulton Archive/
Getty Images; 31 top: Hulton Collection/Getty Images; 31 bottom: Rue des Archives/The Granger
Collection; 31 center top: Apic/Getty Images; 32 background: Hulton Archive/Getty Images.

Maps by Mapping Specialists

Sources:
page 13: Klemash, Christian. How to Succeed in the Game of Life. Kansas City, MO: Andrews
McMeel Publishing, 2010, p. 119.
page 23: Vickery, Donald M., M.D. Live Young, Think Young, Be Young . . . at Any Age: Boulder, CO:
Bull Publishing Company, 2012, p. 285.

TABLE OF CONTENTS

Meet Henry Ford

In the early 1900s, only rich people could afford a car. Henry Ford changed that. He made automobiles that cost less money. Within 20 years, almost anyone could own a car, thanks to Henry Ford.

Henry Ford was born in Michigan on July 30, 1863. He had two sisters and two brothers.

Henry's father wanted him to take over the family farm. But Henry did not like farmwork.

This is a photo of Henry at age three.

CANADA

MICHIGAN
Dearborn
Wayne
County

UNITED
STATES

MEXICO

MAP KEY

● County where Henry
   Ford was born

■ City where Henry
   Ford lived

*Area
enlarged*

Clara Bryant

Ford poses with his son, Edsel, who is about seven in this photo.

Ford was very good
with machines.
He liked to take them
apart to see how they
worked. Then he tried
to make them better.

When Ford was about
25 years old, he
married Clara Bryant.
Five years later,
they had a son
named Edsel.

Building an Industry

The first gasoline-powered automobile was invented when Ford was about 22 years old. He was fascinated by it. About 10 years later, Ford built his own car. He called it the Quadricycle.

10

Ford takes his Quadricycle for a spin in 1896.

When he was about 36, Ford started the Detroit Automobile Company. It eventually failed. But Ford did not give up.

He said, "Failure is simply the opportunity to begin again, this time more intelligently."

This race car, built by Ford in 1902, set a land speed record. It went faster than 91 miles per hour!

13

FORD MOTOR

The Ford Motor
Company in 1906

14

In 1903, Ford started the Ford Motor Company. He designed many **models** of cars. Each was named with a letter—Model A, B, C, and so on.

Each model was better than the one before it. But Ford felt the cars cost too much money. He wanted to make a car that more people could afford.

The Amazing Model T

In 1908, Ford came up with the Model T. It ran well and did not cost much to build. Lots of people wanted one of the cars. Ford had to increase production. He would need a bigger factory.

The Model T was also known as the "Tin Lizzie."

17

New Model Ts roll off the assembly line.

Ford opened a new **plant** in 1910. Three years later, he created a moving **assembly line**. It was the first automobile assembly line in the world. Each Model T moved from one worker to the next on the line. Each worker added a different part to the car until it was finished.

Ford wanted to hire the very best workers. He paid them twice as much as other car companies. People came from all over to work for Ford. They stayed at the company a long time, too.

It took a lot of workers to keep the assembly line moving.

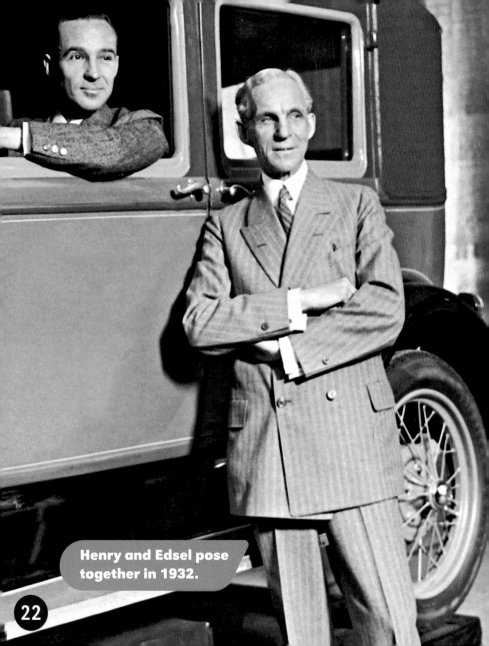

Henry and Edsel pose together in 1932.

New Challenges

In 1919, Edsel took over as president of the company. Henry continued to come up with new ideas, though. He designed the Model A in 1927. He had high hopes for the car. But then something terrible happened.

FAST FACT!

Ford felt it was important to stay busy. He said, "The greatest thing in life is to keep your mind young."

In 1929, America was hit with the Great Depression. Millions of people lost their jobs. Most people had very little money. Fewer people were buying cars than before. By 1932, Ford had to let go of half of his workers.

Hundreds of jobless men line up for free soup.

As Ford grew older, he started having serious health problems. He left the Ford Motor Company in 1945. Very few people saw him after that. Ford died on April 7, 1947, at his home in Michigan.

Ford poses with his wife and grandson in 1946.

Henry Ford made it possible for many Americans to own a car. He was a true **innovator**. He forever changed the way cars and many other products are made.

Timeline of Henry Ford's Life

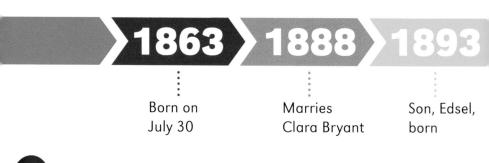

1863	1888	1893
Born on July 30	Marries Clara Bryant	Son, Edsel, born

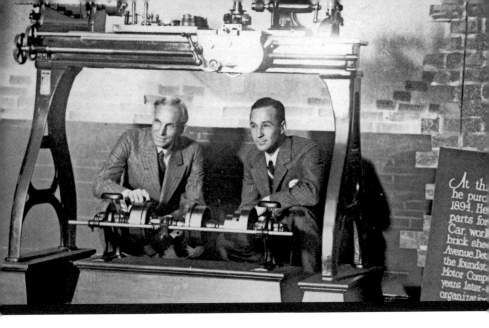

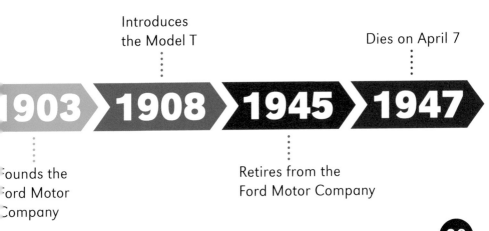

Introduces
the Model T
⋮

Dies on April 7
⋮

1903 > **1908** > **1945** > **1947**

⋮
Founds the
Ford Motor
Company

⋮
Retires from the
Ford Motor Company

A Poem About Henry Ford

Henry Ford cannot be ignored.
He designed some cars folks could afford.
He implemented something fine—
an automobile assembly line.

You Can Be an Innovator

Study the way you do things to see if they can be improved.

Spend your time wisely. Make the most of it!

Make sure the work you do today is just a little bit better than the work you did yesterday.

Glossary

- **assembly line** (uh-SEM-blee LINE): line of workers and equipment along which a product passes until it is complete

- **innovator** (in-uh-VAY-tur): person who comes up with new ideas or inventions

- **models** (MAH-duhlz): particular types or designs of a product

- **plant** (PLANT): buildings and equipment used to make a product; a factory

Index

Facts for Now

Visit this Scholastic Web site for more information on Henry Ford
and download the Teaching Guide for this series:

www.factsfornow.scholastic.com

Enter the keywords Henry Ford

About the Author

Wil Mara has been an enthusiastic "gearhead" since his youth, from racing
bicycles and motorcycles to helping pit crews at New Jersey's legendary
Wall Stadium. He is also a best-selling and award-winning author of more
than 200 books, many of which are educational titles for children.